WHAT DOES A DOCTOR DO?

Felicia Lowenstein

Words to Know

hospital (ha-SPIH-tahl)—A building with doctors, nurses, and equipment to treat sick people.

healthy (HEL-thee)—Being well, not sick.

germs (JURMZ)—Very small living things that can cause one to become sick.

patient (PAY-shint)—the person being treated.

physician (fuh-ZIH-sun)—Another word for doctor.

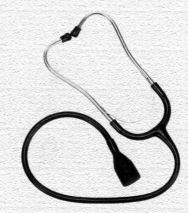

Enslow Elementary
an imprint of
 Enslow Publishers, Inc.

40 Industrial Road   PO Box 38
Box 398   Aldershot
Berkeley Heights, NJ 07922   Hants GU12 6BP
USA   UK

http://www.enslow.com

Contents

The doctor rushed to see his patient.

STAT!

The voice boomed over the
hospital speaker.
"Dr. Niven STAT to Room 111."

Dr. Niven was eating lunch. He
did not even take another bite.
He knew that STAT meant right
away. A child was sick. It was his
job to help. He moved quickly.
He wanted to make it in time.

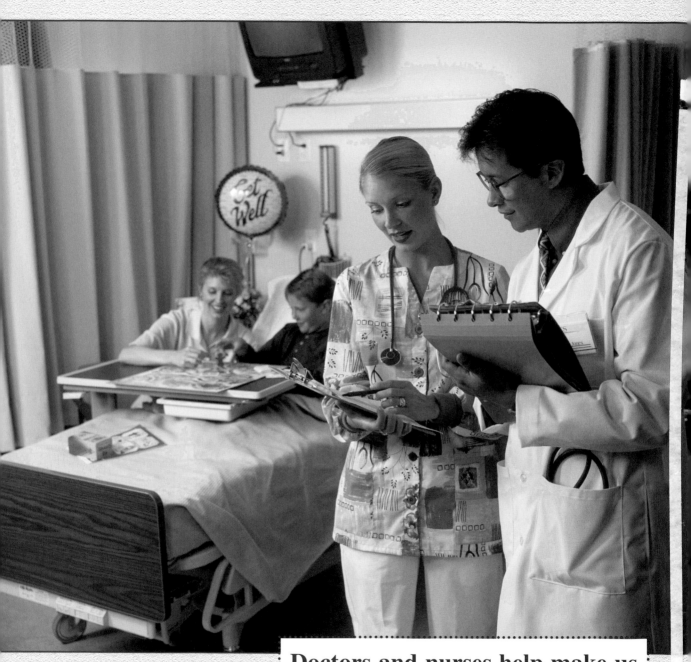

Doctors and nurses help make us feel better when we are sick.

Taking Care of Us

Dr. Niven is a physician. That is another word for doctor. Doctors take care of us. When we are sick, they help us to feel better. They give us medicine. They are part of the team that keeps us healthy.

Doctors go to school for a long time. They learn about the human body.

Do You Want to be a Doctor?

Do you want to be a doctor? If you do, you have to be good in science and math. You have to like to study. Doctors study for a long time. Becoming a doctor needs more training than almost any other job. It takes about eleven years.

Doctors wear name badges.

What Does M.D. Mean?

Look at the doctor's name. The two letters, M.D., mean Medical Doctor. That tells you the doctor went to medical school. He worked in a hospital. He passed a test. He knows all the right things to be your doctor.

eye chart—The doctor uses an eye chart to find out how well you can see.

otoscope—An otoscope helps a doctor see into your ears.

tongue depressor—The doctor uses this to press your tongue down when looking in your mouth.

blood pressure cuff—This is used to check how hard your heart is pumping to move blood through your body.

stethoscope—A stethoscope lets the doctor listen to your heart and lungs.

thermometer—A thermometer will tell the doctor if you have a fever.

reflex hammer—The doctor taps your knee with this to test your reflexes. The doctor wants to see if your leg kicks out on its own.

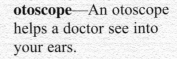

A Doctor's Tools

Doctors have special tools. Doctors use these tools to make sure our body is working well. Take a look.

These doctors work with people's insides.

This doctor works in a hospital.

This doctor works with babies.

Different Jobs

Did you know that not all doctors do the same job? Some work only with children. Some help mothers have babies. Others work with people's insides. There are many jobs. Each doctor has learned his or her special job.

This doctor studies germs.

This doctor hands out medicine.

Where Do Doctors Work?

Doctors work in different places, too. Some work in a hospital. Others work in a doctor's office. Still others work for companies that make medicines. Most doctors work with nurses and other health workers.

This doctor cares for his patient.

When Do Doctors Work?

It seems that a doctor's work is never done. They work long hours. They work in the middle of the night. Even on their days off, doctors may be "on call." That means they have to come in if they are called.

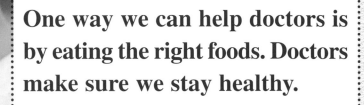

One way we can help doctors is by eating the right foods. Doctors make sure we stay healthy.

Staying Healthy

Doctors keep us safe and healthy. But they need our help too. We can take care of our bodies. We can get enough sleep. We can eat healthy foods. We visit our doctor when we are feeling fine, too. This way doctors make sure we stay healthy.

Wash Up!

Germs are everywhere. Some germs are good. But most are bad. Germs can make us sick. One way to stay healthy and get rid of germs is to wash our hands.

When Should I Wash Up?

After:
  Using the bathroom
  Blowing or wiping your nose with a tissue
  Playing with pets and animals

Before:
  You touch food
  You eat
  You touch your eyes, mouth, or nose

How Do I Wash My Hands?

1. Wet your hands with warm water.
2. Apply some soap.
3. Rub your hands together to make soapy bubbles. Sing your favorite song for 20 seconds.
4. Make sure you wash between your fingers and on the tops and bottoms of your hands. Get your wrists soapy, too!
5. Rinse well.
6. Dry carefully using a cloth towel or paper towel.

For more tips on how to wash your hands, check out "The Buzz on Scuzz" Web site on the next page.

Learn More

Books

Adamson, Heather. *A Day in the Life of a Doctor.* Mankato, Minn.: Capstone Press, 2004.

Liebman, Dan. *I Want to be a Doctor.* Toronto, Canada: Firefly Books, 2000.

Radabaugh, Melinda Beth. *Going to the Doctor.* Chicago, Ill.: Heinemann Library, 2003.

Schomp, Virginia. *If You Were—A Doctor.* New York: Benchmark Books, 2001.

Swanson, Diane. *The Doctor and You.* Toronto, Canada: Annick Press, 2001.

Internet Addresses

Going to the Doctor for Check-Ups
<http://www.aboutchildrenshealth.com/doctor.htm>
You feel fine. Why do you need a doctor? This site tells what happens during a check-up, and why.

"The Buzz on Scuzz"
<http://www.bam.gov/survival/handwashing.htm>
Learn more tips on hand washing on this Web site.

Index

Note to Teachers and Parents: The *What Does a Community Helper Do?* series supports curriculum standards for K–4 learning about community services and helpers. The Words to Know section introduces subject-specific vocabulary. Early readers may require help with these new words.

Series Literacy Consultant:
Allan A. De Fina, Ph.D.
Past President of the New Jersey Reading Association
Professor, Department of Literacy Education
New Jersey City University

Enslow Elementary, an imprint of Enslow Publishers, Inc.

Enslow Elementary® is a registered trademark
of Enslow Publishers, Inc.

Copyright © 2005 by Enslow Publishers, Inc.

All rights reserved.

No part of this book may be reproduced by any means
without the written permission of the publisher.

Library of Congress Cataloging-in-Publication Data

Lowenstein, Felicia.
    What does a doctor do? / Felicia Lowenstein.
        p. cm. — (What does a community helper do?)
    Includes bibliographical references and index.
    ISBN 0-7660-2542-X
    1. Physicians—Juvenile literature. I. Title. II. Series.
    R690.L67 2005
    610.69—dc22
                                        2004006955

Printed in the United States of America

10 9 8 7 6 5 4 3 2 1

To Our Readers:
We have done our best to make sure all Internet Addresses in this book were active and appropriate when we went to press. However, the author and the publisher have no control over and assume no liability for the material available on those Internet sites or on other Web sites they may link to. Any comments or suggestions can be sent by e-mail to comments@enslow.com or to the address on the back cover.

Illustration Credits: Hemera Technologies, Inc. 1997–2000, pp. 2, 12 (thermometer, otoscope, tongue depressors), 22; © JupiterImages, pp. 1, 4, 6, 8, 12 (stethoscope, eye chart, reflex hammer, blood pressure cuff), 16 (top right and bottom right), 20 (all); RubberBall Productions, pp. 10, 12 (center), 14 (all), 16 (left), 18 (all).

Cover Illustration: © JupiterImages (bottom); top left to right (© 2004 JupiterImages, RubberBall Productions, © 2004 JupiterImages, © 2004 JupiterImages).